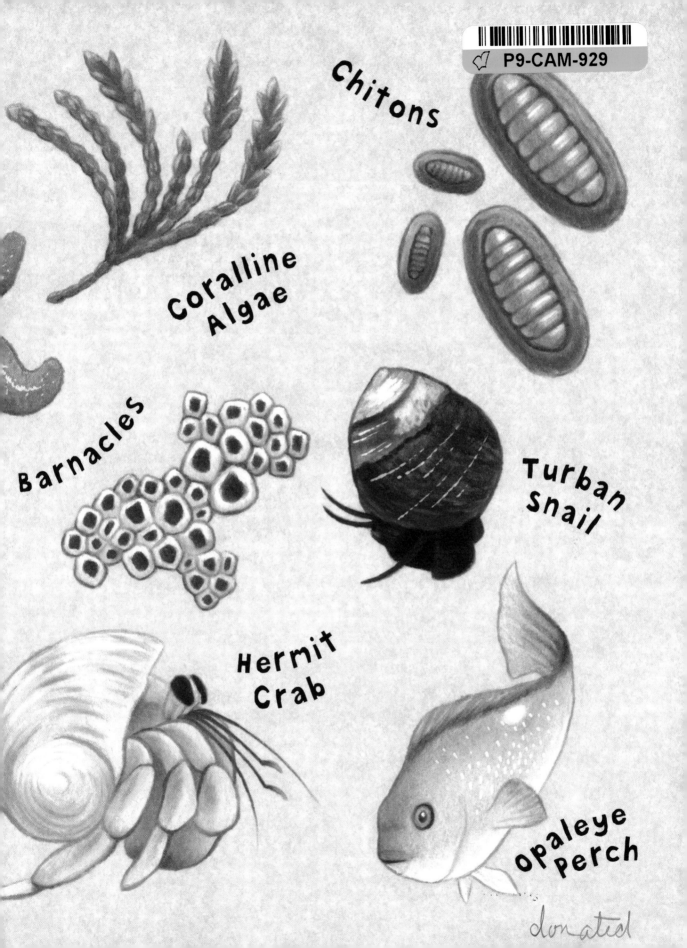

Chitons

Coralline
Algae

Barnacles

Turban
Snail

Hermit
Crab

opaleye
Perch

Pocketmouse at Crystal Cove

Written by Marian Parks

Illustrated by Melinda Beavers

CRYSTAL COVE STATE PARK
LAGUNA BEACH, CALIFORNIA

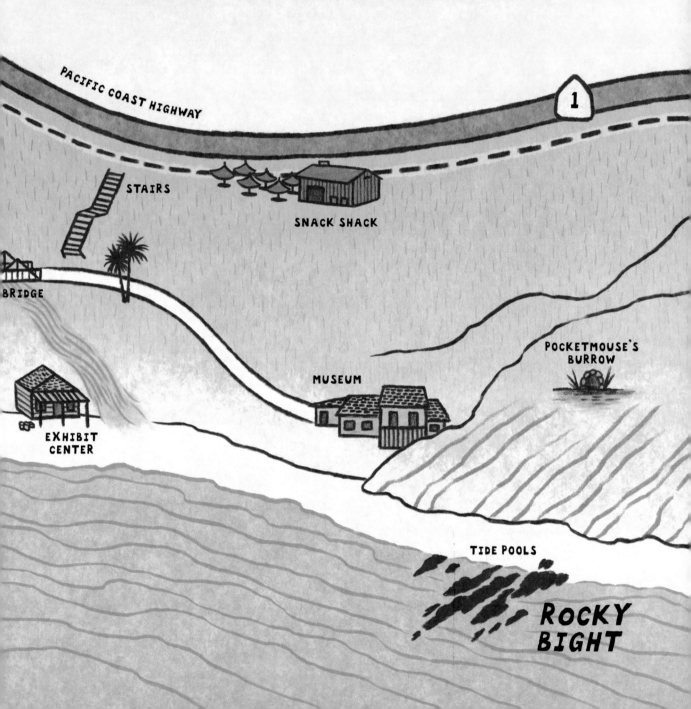

PACIFIC COAST HIGHWAY

1

STAIRS

SNACK SHACK

BRIDGE

POCKETMOUSE'S BURROW

MUSEUM

EXHIBIT CENTER

TIDE POOLS

ROCKY BIGHT

On Crystal Cove Beach lived little Pocketmouse.
He lived all alone in his cozy beach house.
As the sun waved goodbye to each passing day,
He'd watch the stars rise in the vast Milky Way.

When the moon gave a nod that the night had begun,
He'd kick up his heels for some seed-hunting fun.
He'd wiggle his whiskers and sniff with his nose,
Searching for seeds where the wild grass grows.

He walked among plants in the coastal sage scrub,
Smelling lemonade berry and fresh buckwheat shrub.
Pocketmouse loved his California beach home,
But was puzzled whenever he'd forage or roam.

He'd see families of bats, brown pelicans, quail,
Ground squirrels, and coyotes near his hunting trail.
Gophers and rabbits burrowed into the ground,
But never another pocket mouse had he found.

He said to himself, "There have to be others!
Where are my parents, my sisters, and brothers?"
On a branch up above was his best friend Hi Q,
An observant owl, so he asked if he knew.

Hi Q said, "There were pocket mice on the shore,
But after the storm they weren't there anymore.
You were too young to remember the storm,
Or how you survived and kept yourself warm."

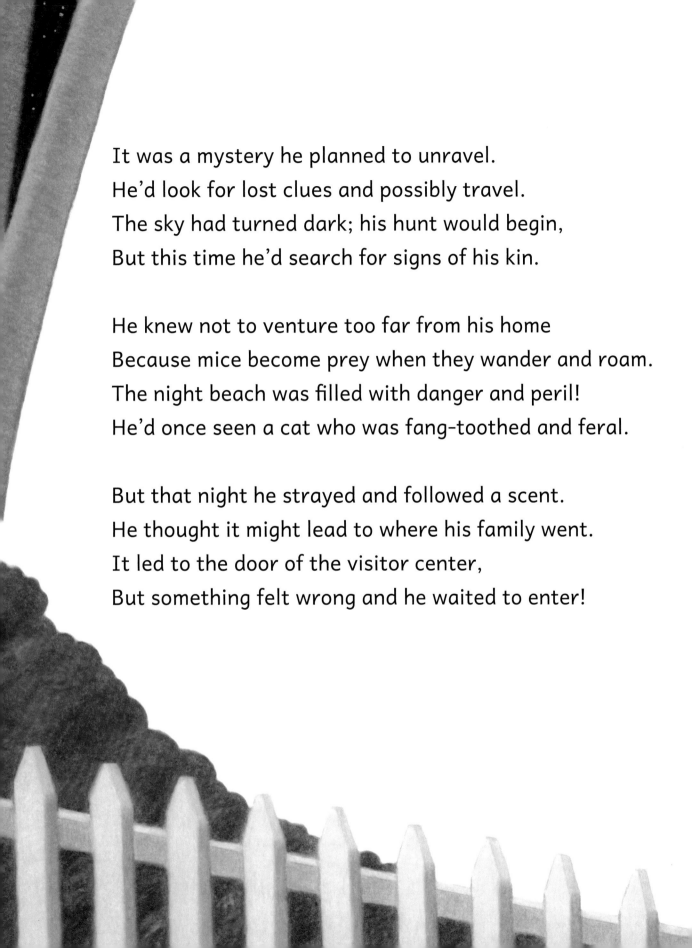

It was a mystery he planned to unravel.
He'd look for lost clues and possibly travel.
The sky had turned dark; his hunt would begin,
But this time he'd search for signs of his kin.

He knew not to venture too far from his home
Because mice become prey when they wander and roam.
The night beach was filled with danger and peril!
He'd once seen a cat who was fang-toothed and feral.

But that night he strayed and followed a scent.
He thought it might lead to where his family went.
It led to the door of the visitor center,
But something felt wrong and he waited to enter!

He heard something stir. He quickly looked back.
A crouched, vile beast was poised to attack!
Pointy fangs flashed—like those of a bat!
Pocketmouse recognized the fang-toothed, feral cat!

His heart raced and thumped. He trembled with fear.
He had to escape! Pronto! High gear!
He squeezed under the door and soared like a rocket.
Gliding to safety in a coat with a pocket.

The pocket was lush with a salty, beach smell,
Like wild grass seed mixed with blue mussel shell.
Pocketmouse thought, "I've smelled this before."
Then he burrowed his head and started to snore.

He awoke to a voice kind and eager to teach
Kids about tide pools and shells on the beach.
Squeals of laughter and joy rang out as she taught
About a sea star and the food that it caught.

She knew about sea snails and barnacles too.
Did she know about mice? Might she have a clue?
Had Miss Waters seen other pocket mice?
Oh, how he wanted to get her advice!

He lifted his head trying to stay out of view,
But he saw her smile and realized she knew.
She saw him hiding, but she looked like a friend.
He felt she was someone on whom he could depend.

His eyes soon adjusted to the striking bright light.
The beach in the daytime was a brilliant new sight.
The colors were vivid—palm trees green as key limes
That swayed in the breeze like musical chimes.

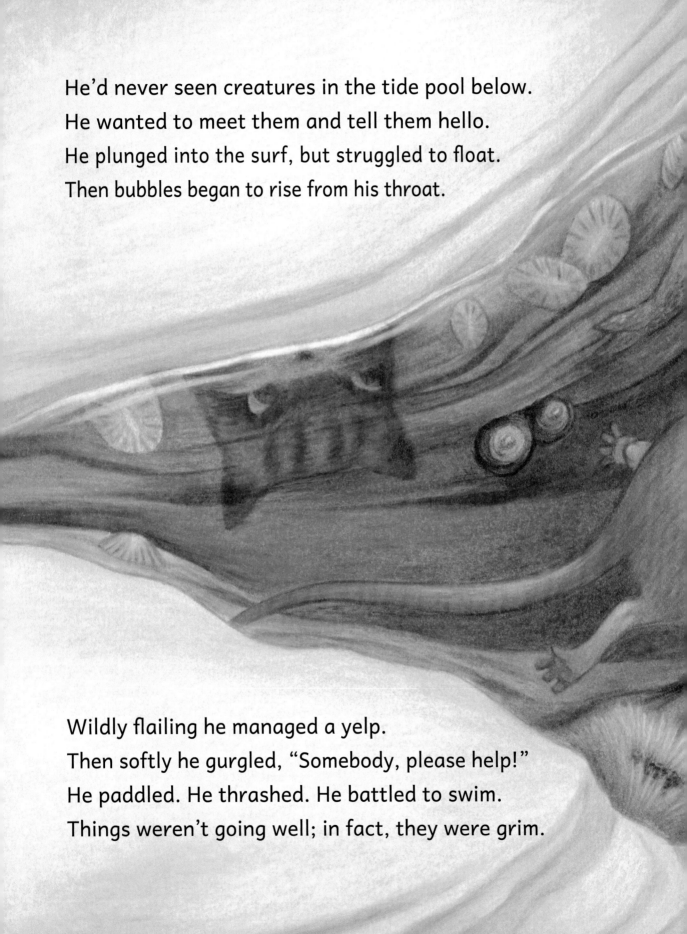

He'd never seen creatures in the tide pool below.
He wanted to meet them and tell them hello.
He plunged into the surf, but struggled to float.
Then bubbles began to rise from his throat.

Wildly flailing he managed a yelp.
Then softly he gurgled, "Somebody, please help!"
He paddled. He thrashed. He battled to swim.
Things weren't going well; in fact, they were grim.

He couldn't escape; the tide was now surging.
A crab was irate and quickly emerging.
But just as he felt water filling his ears,
He heard from the children a chorus of cheers.

Miss Waters leaned over and gently retrieved
Pocketmouse from the tide pool and all were relieved.
She held him quite close; he was cold and afraid.
Then she told a story like a sweet serenade.

"Pacific pocket mice are endangered and rare;
Many have vanished like our state's grizzly bear.
But this little guy—Pocketmouse is his name—
Persevered and survived when a mighty storm came.

He hid in my pocket on the night of the storm.
He needed shelter and a place to stay warm.
Frantic mice scurried all over the shore;
I'm sure it was Pocketmouse they were all looking for."

"When the storm passed and dawn brought us light,
I took Pocketmouse back, so they'd reunite.
But their habitat changed; erosion took place;
His family had fled without leaving a trace.

They may have moved to a place safe and new.
Perhaps to a bluff with a fine ocean view."
Pocketmouse listened to all that she said,
And believed that his kin were alive and not dead.

MS. WATERS

He planned to find them. He'd follow their trail,
With his keen sense of smell, he was sure to prevail.
He'd make a compass and map out his route,
And when spring arrived, he'd start his pursuit.

He heard Miss Waters now speaking again.
He'd only been thinking of finding his kin.
He perked up his head, so that he could hear,
As she spoke softly in his shivering ear:

"It was a sad day for me when I let you go,
To hunt on your own, so you'd thrive and grow.
When darkness set in you'd forage all night,
And each morning I'd see if you were all right."

She told how she watched him and deeply admired,
His friendships, his spirit, and how he inspired.
She told of his courage when left in the wild.
She said that she loved him. And Pocketmouse smiled.

For all those who preserve our parks and protect wildlife
—and for Stephanie, who treasures Crystal Cove.

—M.P.

Nature Tale Books, Inc.
Livermore, California
www.NatureTaleBooks.com
Sales@NatureTaleBooks.com

LCCN: 2015904103

Summary: While trying to solve a mystery, an endangered
Pacific pocket mouse perseveres in his California coastal habitat.

Story themes: Endangered species | Habitat | Nature

Hardcover ISBN: 978-1-943172-00-9

Illustrations were created in colored pencil with
digitally composited and colored details
by Melinda Beavers.

Printed in USA
10 9 8 7 6 5 4 3 2 1

Nature
Tale Books

Visit Our Website for
Common Core Activities
www.NatureTaleBooks.com

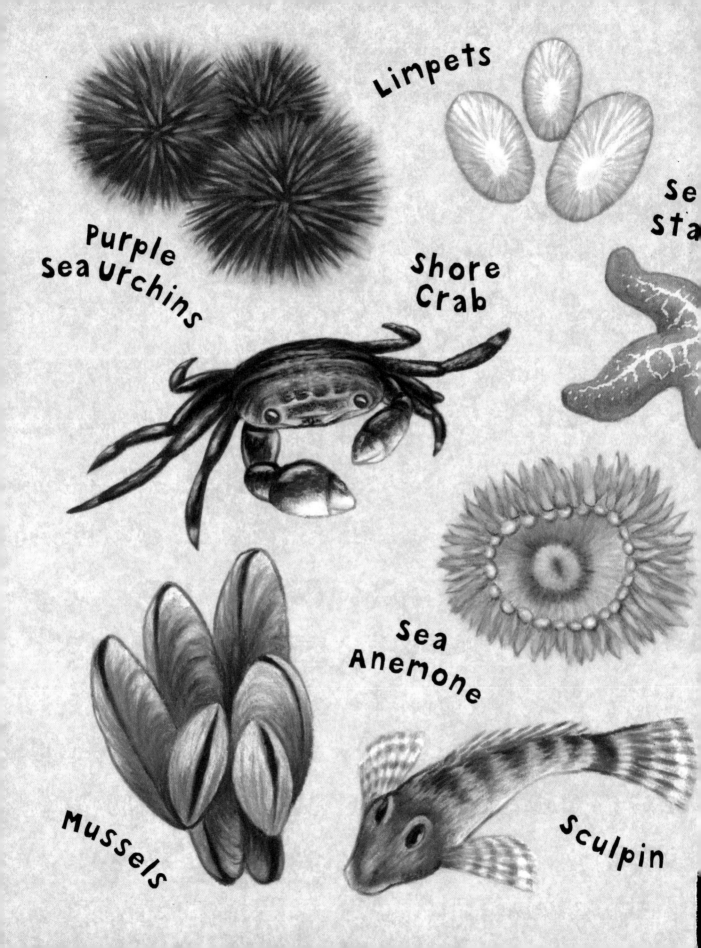

Purple Sea Urchins

Limpets

Se Sta

Shore Crab

Sea Anemone

Mussels

Sculpin